GOING UP WITH GROVER

A COUNTING BOOK

By Linda Hayward
Illustrated by Tom Leigh

A SESAME STREET/GOLDEN PRESS BOOK

Published by Western Publishing Company, Inc.,
in conjunction with Children's Television Workshop.

Hello, everybody! I do not have time to stop and chat because I, Grover the elevator operator, am late for work.
One. . . . Going up!

Good morning, sir.
Two. . . . Going up!

Step right in, please.
Three. . . . Going up!

Watch the closing doors.
Four. . . . Going up!

Step lively, please.
Five. . . . Going up!

Move to the back.
Six. . . . Going up!

What a busy day.
Seven. . . . Going up!

Good morning to you, sir.
Come on, everybody! Make room!
Eight. . . . Going up!

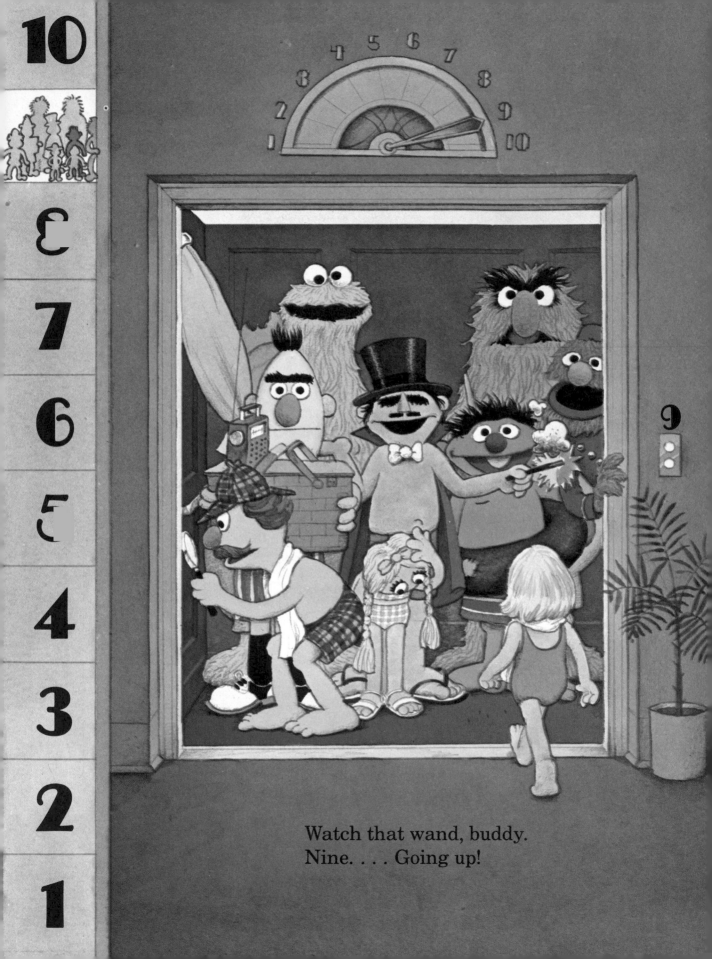

Watch that wand, buddy.
Nine. . . . Going up!

Oh, my goodness!
Ten. . . . Going up!

Swimming pool!
Everybody off!
PHEW! Time for my break.

Closing time.
Going down!

Ten. . . . Going down!
Hey, watch it!

Nine. . . . Going down!
Excuse me, sir, but you are
dripping on my foot.

Eight. . . . Going down!
Have a nice evening.

Seven. . . . Going down!
Maybe I should have been
a bus driver, instead.

Six. . . . Going down!
I thought that marching
band music would never stop.

Five. . . . Going down!
Nice hat, miss.

Four. . . . Going down!
This has been a very
long day.

Three. . . . Going down!
Watch the closing . . . doors, sir.

Two. . . . Going down!
Oh, my!

One. . . . Going up!